Penny Stocks

&

Options Trading

2 Manuscripts

A Beginner's Guide to Earning Passive Income with Penny Stocks & Options Trading

T. Whitmore

Copyright © 2016 by T. Whitmore All Right Reserved.

No part of this publication may be reproduced, distributed, or transmitted in any form or by any means, including photocopying, recording, or other electronic or mechanical methods, or by any information storage and retrieval system without the prior written permission of the publisher, except in the case of very brief quotations embodied in critical reviews and certain other noncommercial uses permitted by copyright law.

Table of Contents

Introduction

CHAPTER 1 - INTRODUCTION TO PENNY STOCK INVESTING

CHAPTER 2 - RISKS ASSOCIATED WITH PENNY STOCK TRADING

CHAPTER 3 - BASIC PENNY STOCKS KEY INDICATORS AND HOW TO LEVERAGE ON THEM

CHAPTER 4 - HOW TO AVOID BEING A VICTIM OF PENNY STOCK SCAMS

CHAPTER 5 - HOW TO INVEST IN PENNY STOCKS

CHAPTER 6 - PROVEN TIPS TO HELP YOU MAKE PROFITS FROM YOUR PENNY STOCKS

CHAPTER 7 - HOW TO LOCATE PENNY STOCK COMPANIES WITH FUTURE WORTH

CHAPTER 8 - SELF ANALYSIS

CHAPTER 9 - CHOOSING A COMPATIBLE BROKER

CHAPTER 10 - PENNY STOCK PLATFORMS

Conclusion

Introduction

Contrary to the belief of many, becoming rich is not as difficult as many people assume it to be. There are several methods through which many people become rich today. Some methods are legitimate while some methods are illegal. Unfortunately too, some methods have a combined play out of legitimate and fraudulent engagements. Off course, there is nothing like half way legitimate and halfway illegal. Having all round legitimate income is definitely possible.

Have you ever come in contact with the idea of buying and selling Penny Stocks? This is one great method used by many today in maximizing their wealth creation potentials. You can also do the same. If you are completely new to this idea, you are on the right page. Having a good understanding of penny stock buying and selling is a good place to start.

My major goal with this book is to help people achieve their goals of becoming rich via the buying and selling of penny stocks. As minute as penny stocks are, many have been recorded to have made huge successes from buying and selling penny stocks.

Riches are not meant for some particular sets of people. Even if we were to agree with this notion, one major fact is that overtaking is definitely allowed in the race to riches.

If you do not know about penny stock trading, especially in this present day, there is very little you can do with your desire to get rich. Do not get me wrong. This is not an insinuation that getting rich has to do with being a genius. Absolutely not! Getting rich with Penny stock trading does not require some high levels of expertise. All that is needed is discovering and practicing some few basic principles that will surely guarantee success.

However, this does not mean that this guide is meant for everyone. There is the need to go beyond desiring to working out the right steps. If you are looking for some instant make rich magic bullet, then I am sorry to disappoint you. You won't find any in this book. What you will find are proven and tested precepts regarding how to succeed in penny stock trading.

CHAPTER 1 - INTRODUCTION TO PENNY STOCK INVESTING

What are Penny Stocks?

Based on the US SEC definition of Penny Stock, this term refers to a security which does its trading at rates below $5 per share. They are, in most cases traded by small companies and individuals. In UK, Penny Stocks are referred to as Penny shares. They are stocks with their prices under £1. In some other countries, penny stocks are referred to as cent stocks. Obviously as may be observed, they do not have a listing on a country's national exchange neither do they meet other specified criteria. They are, basically, very common or ordinary shares that belong to small or public companies whose per share offerings are on the very low scale.

With most penny stocks, a low market pricing rate will inevitably result in low market capitalization. These types of stocks have the tendency to be very volatile. Stock promoters can manipulate stock scenarios to their selfish advantages. Investors are at a higher risk, especially as they are being lured by fast profit fantasies. In the US, trading of Penny stocks are done on the OTC Bulletin boards, over the counter or via pink sheets. They could also be traded on security exchange platforms. These include foreign exchange securities as well as exchanges.

Penny stocks by definition, may also include the securities of some private companies/organizations that do not have trading platforms which could be considered as active

How Penny Stocks are created

Penny stocks are like all other publicly traded stocks. They are created via a process referred to as IPO or initial public offering.

The first step towards creating stocks is that a company files a registration statement with the SEC (Securities and Exchange Commission). Secondly, State Securities laws within the locality of the intended place of stock sales should be observed. After registration approval, the company is licensed to begin sending out orders from investors. The company can then apply to have the stock put up on an exchange platform, trade on OCT or over the counter market.

Another Method is the stock issuing procedure. Small companies make use of this process most times as a means of raising capital to help them grow their business. Although the process is quite lengthy as it involves some very cumbersome levels of paper work accompanied by huge costs, it is however, very efficient. Penny stocks are usually the result of those kinds of ventures. They have potentials for profitability and very risky for investors as well. The first step to take is to hire an underwriter. This is usually an attorney or an investment bank that specializes in Security offers

A company's offer has to be registered either with SEC or a filed registration under Regulation D. This is if exempted. However, if the company needs to be registered, a registration statement form needs to be filed with SEC. This is accompanied by the company's financial statements and other disclosure documents. The financial statements and disclosure documents are to be available for public review as well.

The Company should also ensure it files in prompt and timely reports with SEC. This will ensure that the public offering is maintained. As soon as approval from SEC has been received, the company can then proceed to soliciting for orders for shares from the public.

After initial orders are collected and stock is sold to investors, trading registered offers can proceed. Trading can be done in a secondary market such as a listing on an exchange platform like NASDAQ and NYSE or other over the counter trade medium. Several penny stocks end up being traded on over the counter mediums. This is due to the very strict requirements for listing stocks on larger exchange platforms. In most cases, penny stocks do not meet these requirements. The companies are also not able to afford the huge costs and regulatory process involved.

In some cases, companies make an additional alternative market offering aside from the IPO. Although this step dilutes the existing shares, it however gives the company access to more investors as well as an increase in capital. It is therefore very important that companies who are in the penny stock issuing category bare this is mind. They must work in such a way that they are able to acquire value in the shares as they trade in the open market.

Also, it is compulsory for the companies to continue to publicly provide financial statements as they're constantly updated in order to keep investors informed. They are also able to maintain the ability for over the counter bulletin board quoting.

CHAPTER 2 - RISKS ASSOCIATED WITH PENNY STOCK TRADING

Difficulty Posed by Infrequency

This difficulty is posed mostly to stocks that are already owned. Once they become owned, trading them off becomes difficult. Not only this, trading such stocks become irregular as owners may not find good opportunities with beneficial quotations to trade them. The irregularities posed are the major reasons they may be used to exploit illegal potential gains from investors.

Speculative Investment

Trading penny stocks are purely speculative. This poses huge risks on investors. Investors have no choice but to prepare for win or lose situations. They can lose their entire investment to wrong speculations.

Low or Lack of Liquidity

This is another major risk for investors. Take for example; an investor decides to buy some shares with penny stocks that he likes. What might not be evident at face value is the daily average of trading volumes per time. If this is low, it poses huge risks to the investor when the stock is to be sold. If there are potentials for profitable sales, an investor may decide to place them up for sale. Because of the liquidity risks, there is no guarantee that there will be a ready buyer at the price offered. An investor is then left with two options -either bring down the price or wait for another opportunity. With the first option, profit margin will be low or even worse. The second option can create a bigger problem of being trapped in a pump and dump scheme where all investments are cleared out within a very short time.

Low level Research Capability

Penny stock trading is completely different from other forms of financial trading. It is not like the stocks that are being traded on other major exchange platforms. This is why they have very little or no following. There is almost no penny stock information presented on financial Medias. Analysts don't waste their time with such stocks. This is actually a cause for concern and curiosity. Why is the disposition towards penny stock investment so low or negative?

Wild and Violent Swings

Penny stocks are popular for their wild swinging capacities. There can be severe changes within minutes to few hours of transactions. Investors can swing from highly promising profits to very devastating loses within minutes. For this reason, investors need to spend several hours per day watching their stocks so that they do not have to suffer very devastating disappointments.

AVOIDING PENNY STOCK RISKS

An investor who wants to always be on the winning side needs a very important attribute - the ability to do your own research consistently and come up with information that will make things easier for you while guaranteeing your profit potentials.

Ensure you make your research on virtually every aspect and any aspect of the company you will like to trade in. Research the company history, financial history, management, mission, products and or services, future prospects for the company, etc.

If you happen to be doing your trade online, it is very much advisable to ensure that your transactions are carried out on a private computer. Ensure your network and passwords are strictly confidential and protected.

Insider Trading

Although there are several problems associated with this method, it is a great method for risk avoidance. The ability to study and interpret previous explicit information gives investors access to the actual intentions attached to insider trading. First, remember this - those involved in this form of trading are humans. Do not make the mistake of assuming they do have access to all of a company's secrets. This however does not mean that the attempt to get involved with the insider trading and traders should be carried out carelessly. Since there have been several attempts at following insider trading activities, it has been observed that the insiders tend to be aware that their actions are being monitored. As a result, they tend to be more discrete with their activities thereby making it more difficult to access their information. Because it is illegal to carry out trading activities based on internal information received but was not made public, it is good to be watchful to observe any little information dropped. There is every tendency that there would be large scale sales and purchases after there has been a press release. As an investor therefore, it is important to look out for these signs and act accordingly.

Volume Warning Signals

There are some tips that can help in understanding the swings in stocks especially regarding the volume of transactions. A basic rule to this effect is that high volumes that are losing out on daily basis should be sold off quickly before huge, unredeemable losses occur.

MICROCAP FRAUDS

Most microcap stocks are penny stocks. Microcap stock frauds are forms of security frauds involving stocks acquired via microcap companies. In the United States, they are generally defined as stocks with a market capitalization of less than $250 million. Its predominance is estimated as running into billions of dollars each year.

Generally, microcap stock frauds occur among stocks which are traded on OCT bulletin boards as well as Pink sheets. Obviously, these are stocks that are not listed on stock exchanges because they do not meet the requirements for being listed on the stock exchange. Several types of investor frauds are listed under microcap frauds:

Pump and Dump Schemes

This is called 'Pump and dump scheme' because it is a form of microcap stock fraud.

As have been mentioned before, penny stocks basically trade for very small amounts. These amounts are further categorized into small, smaller and smallest. In most cases, penny stocks which are found in the lowest categories e.g. fractions of a cent are very thinly traded.

These have every tendency of becoming targets of manipulation. Stock promoters often make use of these are baits for unsuspecting investors. These stock manipulators in most cases, first purchase very large amounts of stocks, then inflate the share pricing artificially. This is done by falsely misleading investors with positive statements regarding the falsely inflated shares.

 In the past, scammers used to make use of calls. But nowadays, the internet has provided cheaper and easier methods. Scammers are able to reach to more people thereby making more money.   In sophisticated levels of frauds, individuals and even organizations buy millions of shares. They make use of mediums such as newsletters, stock messaging boards, chat rooms, bulk emails, fake press releases, etc., to push up their stock interest levels. Unfortunately, results have shown that the rise in the use of internet and social medias have created an expansion in penny stock scams.

In most cases, the perpetrator will make people believe that they have based their offers on insider information. Based on the information they have, they know it is best for investors to take advantage of the moment. The best moment for a result oriented investor to buy shares, according to them is 'now'. This creates high levels of rush. Investors get carried away in the process. Buying pressure becomes intense. This pressure pushes up share prices. This rise in prices entices more people and makes them believe in the hype. They then respond by also buying shares as well. When the manipulators see that their 'pumping' scheme has gained a firm hold on people and much stock has been bought, they decide to commence their 'dumping' when they sell off their holdings. They sell off these over priced stocks. As soon as they are done with sales, prices fall and Investors lose their money.

Dump and Dilute Schemes

This is a situation in which companies repeatedly place shares for investors to purchase just so that they can consistently wipe away investors resources. Companies who make use of this scheme have a tendency to, from time to time, reverse and split these stocks.

Chop Stock

This is an equity which is usually traded on OTC bulletin boards, pink sheet listings or on the Nasdaq Stock Market. They are purchased for pennies per share and sold by dubious stock brokers to unsuspecting investors at several dollars per share.

Although somehow similar to a 'pump and dump scheme', 'Chop Stock' is slightly different. Brokerages make money from chop stocks in addition to hyping stocks and marketing stocks purchased at very ridiculously high prices.

With chop stock, brokerage firms usually acquire the bulks of stock by purchasing large bulbs of securities which they had negotiated for and purchased at prices well below the market offer.

Before bulk purchase, the perpetrator's stocks usually have very little or no liquidity. After bulk has been purchased, the company's active brokers will then sell the stock to their brokerage clients at the price which they currently place as asking price. The investors who become victims at such times are generally unaware of this.

Short-term and Distorted

This scam works like the pump and dump scheme but on the reverse form. Perpetrators sell their stock after which they begin to spread false and destructive rumors about the company. One of their allegations would be that the company in question is currently facing a big time lawsuit. At his point, the short term sellers would have made money from their short term positions within the company.

Although this type of scam is not only limited to penny stock trades, the spread of destructive News can have very devastating effects on small cap companies than on medium or large cap companies. Investors are therefore advised to ensure they look at the strength of companies they wish to transact with before going ahead to do so. A company's turgidity is of immense importance. A company that is not well established or that is not very successful will be vulnerable to being easily affected by this type of scam. It is therefore best to completely avoid these types of transactions.

One major factor that should be noted is that these systems have the tendency to function for some time. But there are no guarantees for sustainability over long periods of time. Bearing this factor in mind, it is advisable that investments should be done only with companies who operate with SEC and Possess solid balance sheets which reflect revenue and growth in net income.

However, there could still be conditions for speculations. But if this must be the case, an investor must ensure investment is done in one of the major exchange platforms as written within the pages of this book and other quality writings available. The penny stocks presented for sale should be stocks trading for not less than $3 and as much as $5. Potentials for-profit exist more here than there are with penny stocks lower than this. Comprehensive research should therefore be done in order to get the right information to work with.

Penny Stock Potentials

Although unpredictability is a huge risk factor, it is a factor which comes with rewarding potentials. The unpredictable nature of penny stocks is what makes it quite promising. Please note the careful use of the word *potential*. This is intentional because there are possibilities and potentials depending on how an investor choses to view the risks. Some of the positive sides to the penny stock risk coin are discussed below:

Leverage on Opportunities

As much as good information acquisition is virtually a difficult accomplishment as far as the money making financial markets are concerned, when an investor does get hold of a rewarding prospect before other people do, such an investor would be able to leverage extensively on this for his or her own financial benefit. One huge advantage of penny stock trading is the potential to make huge profits from limited investments. The extent of these rewards basically has more to do with how well an investor has been able to choose stocks and how timely the choice has been.

Excellent Learning platform for Newbies

Many investors see penny stocks as a good entry point for them to be able to acquire stakes within prospective companies that are just coming up. When they are able to utilize this platform, they are able to hold on to lucrative potentials before they actually become rewarding results. For investors who are novices or new to financial trading systems, trading in penny stocks is actually a very good place to start. Newbies are presented with direct and practical access to learning about stock markets fundamentals with very little or no commitments. This is one of the major reasons why over time, there has been an increase in investors of all ages and skills, getting involved in penny stock training. Most people see it as a platform for quick grasping of financial training basics.

Rewards in choosing the Right Stocks

As previously highlighted, it is no news that penny stocks are very unpredictable. Stocks can quickly rise to as much as or even higher than 100% of the buying price within a very short time. As much as this is a scary discovery for many, it is actually a cause for curiosity for risk takers. Risk takers are willing to try their hands on the so called unpredictable stocks. There is however huge gains when the right stocks are chosen and chosen at the right time. For good reward potentials, right stocks must be chosen at the right time and sold at the right time. All these interlink to produce good rewards. In order to be able to maximize this potential the following key indicators will make the profit making task much easier and accessible.

CHAPTER 3 - BASIC PENNY STOCKS KEY INDICATORS AND HOW TO LEVERAGE ON THEM

There are several indicators within the financial market for trading penny stocks. These indicators determine how stocks react or respond to market trends. They can help you earn money if you know how to leverage on them to your advantage. In most cases, these are basically patterns and tip offs that make it easy for you to predict penny stocks. They also provide you with insights into when the best time and opportunity comes to buy or sell penny stocks.

Indicators discussed in this section are not the only indicators that exist. In actual fact, there are several indicators. These are few of the basic indicators. The advanced level indicators need more research on the part of investors before they can be applied successfully. However, the more an investor is willing to consistently take the time to look into financial stocks, their histories, and their marketability in general, the better the chances of making the right choices with penny stock investments.

Instability

Penny stocks are very unstable. This has been well emphasized during the course of this book but this is not the point. The instability has its positives too. You can use this to your advantage. What you should take note of are the magnitude, frequency and the cause of instability. These if well interpreted, will assist you in your stock predictions. Studying the historical trend of a stock can go a long way in helping investors get an insight into how common highs and lows occur with the particular stocks and also insight into how large these instabilities are in comparison with past movements. A good way to do this is to monitor the company press releases. Investors can monitor information of stocks climbing high and coming down as released. They can also take note of what was previously announced, what is currently the situation and also what the company foresees in the nearest future. This will inevitably help you stay ahead of the twists and turns. Investors who have this insight are able to take advantage of unusual behaviors because a stock can go back to its usual unstable nature or lead forward to a mouthwatering change in the future.

Maturity

Companies that trade penny stock are mostly young businesses and investors. The idea of growth and the value of such growth are often determined by how far the company has come. In other words, an established company will no longer enjoy or feel comfortable with the instability of penny stock deals. Young and upcoming companies are more prone to these explosions than the mature stable companies.

Young companies have the greatest risks as well as potential benefits. The condition is however dependent on how they have been able to weather the storm of their years of growth. The basic learning insights actually come within those years of baby steps. If a company is able to scale through those tough learning periods, it will be able to transcend into another level with unprecedented growths.

However, there is also a high chance of going bankrupt. The procedure for finding potential winners and losers is a very tricky process. But the ability to identify the size, age and marketplace infiltrations of a company will definitely help.

Spread and Gap bridging

This is basically the difference that exists between the price which has been offered as a bid by a potential buyer and the price which a seller is asking to be paid for the share. In a situation where the asking price is higher than the price bided, a spread might be a good alternative to prevent a complete loss. Take this scenario for example:

Imagine that a stock was placed for sale at $1. No one seemed to be willing to place a bid higher than $0.80. There is a spread of $0.20 and there can be no transaction. If there is a large spread, it will be difficult to sell a stock. Sometimes it is best to take your very little gain so as not to lose further. This is called bridging the gap. Bridge the gap created by the spread so that the stock can be sold sooner rather than delaying further and encouraging chances for devaluation to occur. With spread and gap bridging, an investor can prevent a loss from occurring and even make gains where losses could have occurred.

Acquisitions and Takeovers

Small companies are often prone to issues of merging, take overs and acquisitions. This is usually because these companies struggle with increasing their size and success. While acquisitions and mergers can be either beneficial or devastating, acquisitions by larger companies are usually beneficial to stock values. If two companies that complement each other and have the same kind of management practice merge themselves together, there are good chances of success.

No matter what the situation is or may be the news of a prospective merger or takeover will surely create a buzzing effect on the stock. This will result in huge buying and selling

Penny stock trading is considered very risky because perpetrators often target beginners in investments as well as experienced investors with an appetite for high risks. Penny stocks are very inconsistent. As much as they have been reported to have produced huge gains within few days and even hours, the vast majority recorded just melted away into thin air or traded off on the infrequent category. It is one investment category which investment bodies are very cautious about. This category of stocks has huge risk potentials and functions on the principle of "all" or "nothing". - Investors can lose their entire investments and even more, especially when acquired on margin or alternatively they can win huge moneys.

As the saying goes… Where there are no rules, there are no offences. This same principle governs penny stock trading. There are rules guiding investments. Market regulations become more and more tightened with caution as the speculative tendencies of investments heighten. This is to help eradicate the potentials for dubious acts while also putting in place the most effective rules for safeguarding investors' interests

5 Rules Guiding Penny Stock Trading

As a result of defensible listed problems as well as the several categories of scams meted out on unsuspecting investors over time, penny stocks has been categorized as a form investment that is mostly based on speculations. Financial regulating bodies around the world have rules in place to guide and protect investors' interests. (FINRA) and (SEC) have some specific rules set aside assist in regulating the buying and selling of penny stocks. Every broker/dealer is mandated to comply with these rules. Then and only then can he be considered eligible to carry out any penny stock transactions.

1. **Requirements for Penny Stock Sales**

    Before any transactions can be effected, a dealer is mandated to approve the transaction of the specific penny stock investor. The investor also, must present a written agreement to the dealer for the said transaction. This measure is taken in order that any form of manipulative or fraudulent tendencies can be prevented from occurring in such investments. The act of customer approval is basically to check a client's suitability for such investment. To this end, approval is only expected to be given after a dealer has carried out an adequate assessment of the client's investment experience as well as objectives, based on his or her financial standing.

    Disclosure Document

A broker/dealer is mandated to present a disclosure document to his client. A disclosure document explains the risk factors which are linked with trading in penny stocks, the concepts associated with penny stocks market, rights of clients, duties of the dealer/broker towards the client, possible solutions in the advent of fraud as well as any other information which can be relevant and handy for the client. The broker/dealer must ensure the client is well advised to properly study the document before taking a decision as this will assist him or her in the decision making process.

3. **Bid/Offer Quotation Disclosure Document**

A broker/dealer is mandated to disclose and later, confirm the present quotation prices as well as other related information to the client before a transaction is effected. Not following this rule is considered unlawful. This rule helps the client in keeping track of the price movement within the market.

4. **Compensation Disclosure**

This rule mandates that an investor be made aware of the money which a dealer/broker earns from a particular transaction. Knowing this might help an investor in making a judgment regarding the broker/dealer's motive being selfish or purely to force a transaction

5. **Monthly Accounts Statement**

A broker/dealer is mandated to send a monthly/accounts statement to his client. This statement discloses details like: purchase price, transaction date, number/ identity of each penny stock and estimated market value of the security based on the most recent bids and buying price. Monthly accounts statements must also include and explain the limited market available for the securities, the nature of an estimated price within such a limited market. In a case where there hasn't been any transaction on the client's account for up to 6 months, the dealer/broker would not be mandated to provide monthly statements. However, a dealer/broker is mandated to send written statements quarterly.

CHAPTER 4 - HOW TO AVOID BEING A VICTIM OF PENNY STOCK SCAMS

It is natural to want to go for cheap investment offers. But a wise investor will be very careful with the word 'cheap'. Learning and knowing how to bargain hunt as key is not always successful with financial markets hence it's more than following your instincts. Cheap stocks however are cheap for some good reasons sometimes. Buying penny stock shares can make investors fall into the Hands of companies that will undercut their performances. It is also a true fact that several people may fall into intense fear which leads the market participants into overpricing or underpricing stock. Despite this, it is definitely true as well that the market sure does pretty well with pricing financial assets.

On daily basis, loads of analysts, strategists, money managers and their likes, waddle through and sift through stocks existing in the market. Often times, their research as well as those of millions of investors' place prices on each stock. The prices are often close to what they are worth.

Having laid the above foundations, one can conclusively deduce that penny stock trading is obviously not a practice to be indulged in by new investors or those who have minimal risk tolerance. If you are new to the trade, you do not have to allow all this factors to serve as a discouragement to you. What you must know however is that you need to be willing to take the risk. Be ready at least to stake a little part of your acquisition for what you believe in and want to achieve. Below are some measures which will help you preserve at least, the major part of your trading capital. With some luck on your side, you might even be on the winners' cadre.

Understand the difference between Research Reports and Promotions

From time to time, promoters regularly seek the services of newsletter writers to come up with enticing reports about their stocks. Many of these writers are only particular about what they have been paid to-do which is to make up convincing cases that will entice investors to invest in worthless penny stocks. They expertly weave up their cases using outlandish projections, hyperbolic statements and even deliberately distorted statements in some cases. To this end, a penny stock investor needs to learn to be able to decipher between stock promotion attempts and equity research based on legitimate goals. A good way to go about achieving this is to read and study the section for disclosures at the end of the report. There he or she will find out and know if the writer has some direct compensation for the report that they have written in order to recommend the company. When this is actually the case, the report is basically an advertisement and should not be mistaken for an actual research report.

Management Credibility

The success of a company to a large extent depends on the quality of the management. Penny stock companies have this same as a rule. Although it is not realistic to expect to find a perfect system of management, nonetheless, an investor should still study the management's previous records to observe the trend over time. This will help him observe if the directors and executives have had any significant successes/failures and regulatory/legal matters.

Financial Situation

It is a good thing for an investor to make attempts at getting a good view at a company's financial records in order to have a proper insight into their financial standing. As much as penny stocks generally do not provide in-depth financial information. An investor can seek and obtain the needed information. Intensely scrutinize the balance sheets. Observe if the company has any intensive records of debts or outstanding liabilities. Observe the net cash in hand. Compare recent records with not so recent records. If there has been a consistent high growth in the revenue in recent times, this is a good sign.

Disclosure Quality

Observe the level of disclosure of the company. How willing are they when it comes to disclosing information. The higher the levels of disclosure provided the better. That is an indication of corporate transparency. Obviously, it is best to avoid companies with limited or tight fisted information

Achievable Business Plan

Investors are to carefully evaluate the company business plan. Observe if it is realistic or achievable. Are they truly in possession of the assets that have been declared as theirs or is their declaration a makeup?

CHAPTER 5 - HOW TO INVEST IN PENNY STOCKS

Having learnt how to avoid being scammed, you can confidently move on to the aspect which you must have been waiting for - investing in or purchasing penny stocks. Below are some important guidelines to be considered when buying penny stocks.

How to Buy Penny Stocks

Once you've learned to dodge scammers, here are five steps to follow when purchasing a penny stock.

Upside Potential Evaluation

The reason for your investment is so that you can make profits. The first question you need to ask is if the penny stocks you are about to buy, has an upside profit potential. Your evaluation should be based on reality. If your intended investment is little, you will need to device a realistic reward-risk assessment evaluation for the stock.

Limit Holdings and Diversify

Penny stocks, investments like most investments, require wisdom and prudence. You might be excited about your penny stocks and the potentials you can see in them. However, there is the need to protect you. Reduce potentials for losses by limiting your holdings in the stocks. Your holdings should be from 1%-2% of your entire value.

Furthermore, it is also advisable to diversify with your penny stocks up to a maximum of 5%.-10% of your entire portfolio and depending on how much risk you are willing to take.

Evaluate Liquidity and Trade Volumes

Ensure you have enough liquidity with trading volumes in the stock. This will help you trade efficiently. Even if you have previously made successful investments with your penny stock, you need to bear in mind that you will still need to be able to sell your shares. If this precautionary measure is not taken, there could be situations where there are limited buyers with an extensive bid and asking spreads, thereby making it almost impossible to transform hard profit to actual profits.

Search for stocks that are of high quality

Penny stock companies are the same in terms of value. Some are worth more than others. You know a good venture by its quality. They are set of experienced managers who in most cases have existing track records from their previously successful exited companies.

Ability to know when to buy or Sell your Stock

As much as it is very important to know when and how to buy penny stocks, it is also of utmost importance that you know when and how to sell your stocks. Most penny stocks are not to be bought and held for long term investments. This sector mostly thrives on short term investment basis. For this reason, it is not only very important to know when to buy but to also be able to identify when it's time to sell out your stocks. If you have made some sizeable profits on your penny stock transactions over a short period, it is wise to look at the prospects of booking them off soon rather than wait for some bigger gains that may never surface.

CHAPTER 6 - PROVEN TIPS TO HELP YOU MAKE PROFITS FROM YOUR PENNY STOCKS

The enticing fact about penny stocks is simple. Penny stocks costs very little and promises huge profits. As much as this is true, it is also true that it is a good way to lose your money. As scary as this Clause may be, it has a positive alternative. Penny stocks trading is a good way to make money

So if you find yourself among those who are prepared to delve into the penny stock wealth potentials, here are some proven tips that will help you.

Disregard Penny stock success stories

Do not fall into the mistake of believing the success stories that are spread out everywhere. As have been mentioned before, these are simply promotional gimmicks. Penny stocks investment is not to be embarked upon same way as lotto tickets. Unfortunately, many fall into this error and end up losing again and again. Think of penny stocks like a two faced friend that can't be trusted. Simply focus your attention on profitable penny stocks that have firm meanings and growth and are making as much as 52 weeks highs

Don't Ignore the Disclaimer Sections

Every penny stock promotional mail you receive will most definitely come with a disclaimer section. When you read the disclaimer section, you will see information which tells you that the promoters have been paid. Their goal is therefore to pitch stock since their investors desire the company's exposure. When you read the disclaimer section, you will observe a conflict of interest.

Disregard Tips

In most if not virtually all cases, penny stocks are sold than bought. Most sales or purchases are made through the tips that are sent via Newsletters. The free newsletters you get from time to time are not actually free. Worst still, the tips given to you are not given out of the goodness of the heart. This is not to say giving success tips is wrong but in most cases, the so called tips provided in penny stocks newsletters contain false promises and assurances about their crappy companies. Most newsletters will never tell you the truth. Promoters are simply being paid to embellish. They rarely will tell you when to sell your stock and in most cases, it's too late to do so.

Be Fast in Selling

A beautiful thing with penny stocks is that an investor has the capacity to make as much as 30% within a few days of trading. If you are lucky to make that kind of return, don't wait! Sell quickly!

Unfortunately, losses accompany greed. Many investors become greedy. They aim for very high profits. They forget that they are treading on uncertainty. Recognize that the penny stocks you are into might be pumped before you know it. Be wise! Take any profits on hand and simply move on.

Refuse to Listen to Company's Management or Personnel

As far as the penny stock investment terrain is concerned, do not fall into the trap of believing information you get from companies. You can't afford to trust anyone. The companies are simply trying to inflate their stock so more money can be raised for them to remain in business. There are no dependable business models neither is there accurate data. Most penny Stocks are scams that have been created for the enrichment of insiders. The same caucus of people are the ones who run promotions. They make use of different press releases and companies.

Refuse to Sell Short

Penny stocks are very volatile. It is so easy to lose as much as 50% or even more if on the wrong side of the business. It is very appealing to short pumped up penny stock. However, don't do it. More so, finding shares of penny short is not an easy task especially with the ones that had made huge moves through hyping and newsletters promos. Word of advice... Leave short penny stocks to the experts.

Lookout for penny stocks with high volumes

In your own best interest, it is advisable to look out for stocks which trade at a minimum of 100, 000 shares daily. Trading stocks with low volumes can make you static and unable to rise above your position. Ensure you are conversant with the number of shares traded as well as the dollar volume. Trade penny stocks which are priced at over 50c per share, in order to be on the safer side with your investments. This is because stocks which are trading less than 100, 000 shares daily and less than 50c per share are not considered liquid enough.

Buy only the best of the best

Buy penny stocks that have had good earnings or soaring as high as 52 week in volumes, this is about a quarter of a million shares daily. These are not difficult to find if you look out for them. The only and major challenge is finding stocks that make 52-week highs but not as a result of scams like the pump and dump scheme. It is therefore of utmost importance to be very cautious.

Avoid Trading Large Portions

Many have become bankrupt due to this. As a penny stock investor, you need to be very careful with sizing portions. Refuse to trade big no matter how tempting the offer looks. On the safe side, do not trade more than 10% of your stock daily. Also ensure you limit the size of your shares so you can quickly rid of the stock.

Don't be too overwhelmed with a penny stock

Virtually every penny stock company wants you to think they are offering you the best breakthrough of your life time. Not only you as an individual. The entire world also finds them, indispensable. Enter the world of penny stock trading with some cynical disposition. Ensure you do not go by what you have been told. There is no guarantee that you have been told the entire truth. Do your own research. Diversify with your trading. Penny stock trading has over time earned a bad reputation. You need to be careful.

CHAPTER 7 - HOW TO LOCATE PENNY STOCK COMPANIES WITH FUTURE WORTH

Knowing how to choose good penny stocks from quality companies can make a huge difference between successful trading and failing trade. Here are some tips to help you locate a promising penny stock company.

Trending Companies

Look out for companies that are trending. Consult Investor's Business Daily for listed companies. Then turn to the market section. Run through the list of companies and look out for companies which form the strongest within the list. Select companies with highest (SRI) 'Relative Strength Index'. Companies with high RSI's are in a stronger stock investment trends in comparison with companies with low RSI figures.

Penny Stock Screening

There are some free penny stock screeners available online. You can search for any of these to use in screening the available penny stocks that you find. To do this, begin by selecting OTC as the required exchange. Look for the company heading. You will see a drop down menu, click on and highlight the companies you would like to search. With penny stocks, there are usually low market capitalizations. Make use of a market capitalization within the range of $100 million - $300 million. This method selection will help you sift out weaker stocks. Use 100,000 as your minimum average amount of volumes. Penny stocks are usually traded thinly. This can make closing a trade difficult.

Stock Price range

Consider using a stock price range that will make your work easier. Penny stocks that are trading for less than $0.009 per share can be easily manipulated by fraudsters. While using a price range from 5c to about $2 can help in avoiding such problems. You can also enter positive sales and growth attributes in order to find companies which are earning money. Changing your search criteria will produce a shorter list of qualitative penny stock companies.

Financial Statements

One important factor here is that companies that are transparent will publish their financial records online. You can use search engines like Finance search to search out companies with their financial statements. Study these. Check to see if the company is growing. Also see if sales are increasing. Are per share earnings positive or negative? Does the company have enough cash for its day to day operations? Is the company debt free? Finally, take out a stock chart. Check to confirm that the company is up-trending. Screen all the companies. Screen one company at a time using this method. This will help you find the best penny stocks and companies for you to invest in.

CHAPTER 8 - SELF ANALYSIS

Before setting off in your search for a compatible broker, you need to first analyze your own investing style. Your style in investing is one of the major factors that need alignment with your broker choice. Determining your style is based on your needs. In doing this, try answering these questions realistically:

- Are you in need of advice or you are capable of working on your own with research reports?
- How is your usual trade size?
- How long do you usually hold on to your investments?
- How important is fast and efficient execution of orders to you?
- How important is having a broker you can assess directly to you?

Types of Investor Personality

There are basically four investor personalities discussed here in this book. Try determining the one that best describes you. Check if your broker is able to provide you with services that match your investor personality the most.

Independent investors

This category of investors does not need any form of special assistance or advisory service. They like to carry out their own research thereby empowering themselves. They are quite efficient with the attempts that they make personally. They select their own stocks themselves and place online orders. For this category of investors, speed is a handy attribute. They are fast and consistent in trade execution. They rather go for low commissions than delay trading for huge profits. With this scale of prioritization, they are able to take advantage of the lowest levels of commission. A lot of brokers prefer this class of investors because they make up a large range of market potentials.

Dependent Investors

This category of investors needs assistance. They are not able to take initiatives on their own. They need some holding of the hand and assistance with selecting prospective investment opportunities. This category needs brokers who are experienced in offering individualized advice and assistance. This mostly applies to new investors who most times, need all the assistance they can get when just starting. Obviously, extra services will definitely attract more commission. As more investors become independent, brokers who are involved with this category of investors become scarce and most times, difficult to access. The ones who are regular at this point are usually the larger companies. These are called full service brokers. They provide several services that successful penny stock investments require for success. These include stock picking, tax planning, long and short-term planning, asset allocation, etc.

Daily Investors

These are expert stock traders who hold on to positions for few minutes or few hours maximum. This way, they are able to make and seal off several trade deals per day. Most of the stock trades are taken and sealed off within a day. As a result, daily traders value speed in orders and accomplishing trades. For them, making use of the right broker is as important as the stocks. They place several trades per day. This is why they are able to demand exceptionally low commissions.

Short-Term Investors

These are not same as daily traders. Short-term positions differ. They range from one hour to few months, in most cases. This type is often times used by high ranking investors. They're professionals who have devoted much time to studying and understanding all aspects of trade and investment. Investors in this league need access to advanced research information, excellent execution knowledge, etc. With this height of capability, short term traders obviously do not need assistance from a broker.

CHAPTER 9 - CHOOSING A COMPATIBLE BROKER

Let's be realistic here, you really won't be able to invest successfully without a brokerage account. As a beginner investor in penny or stock trading, choosing a favorable broker will be a different ball game entirely when compared to how an experienced investor would go about choosing one. The process of choosing a broker is not so different from that of choosing penny stocks. This process also requires some careful considerations.

I guess you already know by now that not all brokers are right for every investor. Here in this chapter, I have provided some guidelines to help you choose a compatible penny stock broker who won't leave you penniless.

Who Is a Broker?

A broker is an individual or organization who plays the role of an intermediary between buyer(s) and seller(s). Brokers get paid commissions. A commission is usually a percentage of a client's purchase or sale. Some brokers receive payments of fixed fees per transaction and some receive a mix of both commissions and fixed fees. There are several categories of brokers. But, for the purpose of this book, we shall be looking at the financial broker.

There are basically two classes of financial brokers - regular and resellers. The regular brokers deal directly with their customers. The reseller brokers, on the other hand, are brokers who function as intermediaries between a bigger scale broker and a client.

Regular brokers are considered more reputable than the resale brokers. This is not a pointer to mean that resale brokers are bad or incompetent. However, the fact is that you need to check and observe them critically before choosing to engage their services. Regular brokers are registered members of recognized financial regulatory boards, such as FINRA, etc.

Looking at it from a different angle, one would say, there is a major difference between full-service oriented brokers and discount brokers. As can be deduced, from the name, full service means 'full'. There is the provision for more services

For beginner investors, one could rightly say that discount brokers should be the choice. Considering the cost of the regular broker full offer, making this a choice as a new investor is not financially feasible especially as newbie

CHAPTER 10 - PENNY STOCK PLATFORMS

Over The Counter (OTC)

Over the Counter (OTC) is a phrase used in referring to stocks which are traded through a dealer network and not the centralized exchange platforms are securities traded in some settings different from the usual formal exchange platforms. It also refers to debt securities and financial instruments. For many investors, there is a very small difference that exists between other major exchange platforms and the OTC. The vast developments in electronic quotes and trades have brought about a much higher level of liquidity along with better information availability. However, there are some major differences that exist between all the mediums of transaction. Basically with an exchange, all the parties are exposed to the different offers available from other countering parties. This may not be the case with dealer networks. There isn't enough transparency and also less strict regulations on these exchange mediums. For this reason, amateur investors are liable to taking additional risks which could be subject to unfriendly adverse conditions.

Furthermore, OTC market platforms operate some of the most popular networks like the OTCQX Best Market, Pink Open Market and the OTCQB Ventures Market. In these markets, you find stocks that are unlisted. These are traded on the Over the Counter Bulletin Board (OTCBB), i.e., Pink Sheets. Although, NASDAQ is known to operate as a dealer network, their stocks are generally not classified as OTC. This is because NASDAQ is considered to be a stock exchange platform. Not only that, OTCBB stocks are in most cases either penny stocks or offered by companies with bad or poor credit histories.

Stocks are most times traded on OTC because of the smallness of the company and because they are unable to fulfill the exchange listing requirements. These PP-stocks are also referred to as unlisted stocks. Securities are traded by broker/dealers who canvas with one another directly by phone or internet.

Dealers are like the market makers while the OTC Bulletin Board functions as the inter dealer quotation system providing trading information.

Unlisted Securities

Unlisted Securities are financial instruments which are not traded on an exchange. They are however traded on the Over the Counter platform. They are also referred to as OTC Securities. The facilitation of buying and selling of unlisted securities is mostly done by Market makers within the OTC market. Since they are not traded on exchange, they are often times less liquid than the listed securities.

Listed Securities

These are financial instruments that are traded via an exchange. Examples are NYSE and NASDAQ. As soon as a private company decides to go public in issuing shares, such company will first need to choose which exchange it wants to be listed in. in order to do this, it has to meet the requirements of the exchange listing. The entry and annual listing fees has to be paid as well. Requirements for listings differ based on exchange. They also include a minimum stock holders' equity, minimum number of shareholders and a minimum share price. Furthermore, the listing requirements of exchanges are set in place to ensure that only top quality securities are being traded on the platform. This is to ensure that the exchange's reputation is upheld among investors.

Listing on the NASDAQ is very much cheaper than listing on the NYSE. As a result, newer companies usually opt for the NASDAQ as an alternative when they find that they have been able to successfully meet up with the requirements.

Very importantly, it is important to note that the exchange platform on which a company decides to be listed on has a high tendency to affect the way investors view the stock. Because of this, some companies decide to do a cross listing. They cross list their securities on more than one exchange platform. If for any reason, a stock fails to meet up with the exchange listing's requirements; such stock will be taken off the list. Securities that are delisted are no longer allowed to trade on the exchange platform. Sometimes though, they can be allowed to trade over the counter. Obviously, this is because the over the counter platform does not have any listing requirements.

Exchange

This is a market place where securities, derivatives, commodities as well as all other financial instruments are brought for trade. The main function of an exchange is to bring about and ensure a fair and orderly practice of trading activities. It is also to ensure efficiency in the dissemination of price line information for all the securities that are trading on the exchange. Exchanges provide companies, government organizations as well as several other groups, a favorable platform for the sale of securities to investors.

An Exchange can be a place where traders come to conduct their businesses. It can also be an electronic platform in form of internet and telephones. Also, they can also be share exchange platforms. This depends on the geographical location. Most countries of the world have exchanges practiced. The most prominent ones are found in London, New York, Tokyo, etc.

Wide Electronic Coverage

With the advancement in technological awareness, trading has become increasingly being conducted via electronic devices. Electronic markets are becoming more and more sophisticated such that, many have to keep themselves in line with the flow or simply fall out of the league. The beauty of this is that trading can be done without having to move an inch from the comfort of one's home.

Requirements

There are requirements for participation in an exchange. Companies or groups that wish to participate in offering securities for trade need to meet these requirements before they can be allowed to do so. Requirements are in different forms with some more rigid than others. However, the basic requirement includes provision of regular financial reports, minimum capital requirements and audited earnings report.

Benefits

Stock exchange has several benefits for participants. A stock exchange can be used in raising capital for a company desiring growth and expansion in its operations. Also, exchange provides adequate control of the market platforms and ensures a fair environment for trading to occur.

Pink Sheets

Pink sheets got their name from their color. Pink papers are usually used in printing them. You can check if a company trades on pink sheets. Companies trading pink sheets are recognized with the symbol "PK" which is placed at the end of the stock. Pink sheet securities are traded by investors or brokers with the use of the decentralized OTC markets. Examples are the OTC bulletin boards or OTC link. Both of these are included in the Financial Industry Regulatory Authority (FINRA). There are virtually no restrictions for entering these Securities. OTC links places no restrictions on listed securities either. It is however required that financial reports are updated and properly filed with SEC, insurance regulators and Banking regulators.

OTC Pink

This is the lowest rank of the three market branches available for over the counter stocks as operated by the OTC Markets Group. OTC offers trading within a wide range of equities. This can be done through brokers and companies who have defaulted or are facing financial pain. OTC companies are classified on the basis of information provided by them since there are no disclosure requirements.

OTC Pink companies are quite flexible with their procedures for reporting. As such, classification is based on the quality and quantity of information which is being provided by investors. These are companies with current information, limited information or simply, no information.

Current Information

This category includes companies who follow the international standard of reporting or alternative standard reporting. These ensure they make their fillings available to the public. They provide news services along with their OTC disclosures.

Limited Information

This set includes companies included companies under financial distress, troubled firms, bankrupt companies as well as any other financial or accounting issues. Also included are companies that are not willing to meet the OTC s basic guidelines for disclosure.

No Information

These companies simply do not provide any form of disclosure.

Conclusion

On a final note, it can be rightly concluded that trading penny stocks is a very lucrative wealth creation modality. Trading in penny stocks requires some basic principles. Having an appropriate understanding of these principles and how they are applied goes a long way to determine the achievement of success.

Options Trading

A Beginner's Guide to Earning Passive Income from Home with Options Trading

T. Whitmore

Copyright © 2016 by T. Whitmore All Right Reserved.

No part of this publication may be reproduced, distributed, or transmitted in any form or by any means, including photocopying, recording, or other electronic or mechanical methods, or by any information storage and retrieval system without the prior written permission of the publisher, except in the case of very brief quotations embodied in critical reviews and certain other noncommercial uses permitted by copyright law.

Table of Contents

Options Trading

A Beginner's Guide to Earning

Introduction

DAY 1 Options Essentials

   What is an Option?

DAY 2 Types of Options

   Index Options

   Commodity Options

   Forex Options

   Binary Options

DAY 3 Trading Options

   Placing the Order

   Market Order or Limit Order

   Time Restrictions

DAY 4 Option Pricing

   Pricing Basics

Greeks

   Delta

   Gamma

   Theta

   Vega

Day 5 Buying Selling, Exercising Options

DAY 6 Option Strategies

   Writing Covered Calls

   Selling Naked Puts

   Vertical Spreads

   Calendar Spreads

   Iron Condor

Conclusion

Introduction

In the world of financial trading, options stand alone. It is easy to understand how you can buy and sell shares in the company. It is a slight stretch to understand how you can "short" the things you are trading, selling them before you buy them to make a profit from a reduction in price.

Moving on to derivatives other than options, even these are straightforward.
Things you can buy "deriving" their value from other things, as for example the value of a futures contract changing as the price of the underlying commodity varies, that can be worked with.

But when you get to options trading, while the basic definition is simple the complexity is multiplied. No longer are you looking at a stock which may go say from $51 to $57, thereby simply giving you a profit (or loss) from a $6 move. You are looking at the same stock for which you can pick an option at a price of $45, $50, $55, $60, etc. You also get to pick the date by when you expect the price change to happen. And whether you are bullish or bearish, you can back up your hunch by either buying options, at a cost, or selling them and getting some in- come, though often at a risk as you will see.

This Guide to Options is designed to steer you in the right direction, giving you a full understanding of the many different ways in which you can set up your option trading, and the associated risks and rewards.

I would not advise you to go ahead into options trading on the basis of the information in this book alone. You will however understand the possibilities, and be able to look into the strategies that appeal to you. Unlike some of the entreprene urs rushing out there, I take the time to explain the basics of what you need to know, so you are in a situation to evaluate any further education and experience you may need.

I hope you're not disappointed to find that reading this book alone will not equip you completely for the task, but you must understand that financial trading of any type takes study and work to perform successfully. One idea that you must keep in mind is that on a trading timescale, which is typically days or weeks, you will not see much fundamental shift in the value of most things. So trading profit comes mainly from other traders' losses.

This is clear when trading something like shares, but equally true with derivatives and options. When you take off the commission that your broker or dealer gets in some manner from your trading, you can see that there is less money to go around, and in fact the majority of traders lose. Therefore you have to educate yourself and trade more smartly than the majority of traders to survive and thrive.

Though the basics of trading are (relatively) immutable, you should consider this book simply the start of your option trading education and career. It is my intent to give you the best grounding possible, so that you can look forward to a long and successful vocation.

DAY 1 Options Essentials

What is an Option?

What is an Option?
An option is a guarantee that provides you the right, to either go long or go short on the underlying futures contract at a pre-determined entry price on or before a specific date. Each offers the opportunity to take advantage of price moves in the futures markets without actually having a futures position. Options are available for each futures contract delivery month for up to two years into the future.

There are two types of options, call options and put options. Call and put options are separate option contracts. They are not the opposite side of the same contract. For every call client there is a call agent, and for every put buyer, there is a put seller. The buyer pays a premium to the seller in each transaction.

Call Option
The call option grants the buyer the right, but not the obligation, to go deep on the underlying products futures contract at a pre-specified entry price (i.e., strike price) on or ahead of an expiration date. You would usually buy a call option when you believe that the futures value will grow.

Put Option
A put option provides the purchaser the power, but not the responsibility, to go short on the underlying stock futures agreement at a pre-specified entry cost on or ahead of a particular date. A put option is employed when you consider the futures price will reduce.

Option Buyer
The buyer or holder of an option can choose to exercise their right to hold onto the option until it matures, trade it before it expires, or simply let the option expire.

Option Seller

An options seller is also called the writer. The seller is usually a speculator and is obligated to take the opposite futures position if the buyer exercises their right. In return for the premium, the seller assumes the risk of taking an adverse position.

There are many different types of options when trading depending when, where and who you are trading with. However to understand the basics and get a real grasp on this kind of investing we will keep it simple.

Let us begin with the American option.

American Option - Can be employed at any moment between the time of buying and the expiration date. Most exchange-traded are of this kind.

European Option - The only difference a European option and an American version is that they can only be exercised at the time of the expiration date.

The strange thing is that the American and European moniker have nothing to do with geographical location. It is the just the terms used to distinguish between the two different types.

I'm afraid options get even more complicated. Now we need to look at the other types out there starting with long-term options.

Long- Term Options

When people think about options trading they often only consider short-term options of a couple of months or so. It is possible to have options that can be held for years for long-term investors.

At this point in the financial world, they become what we know as LEAPS (long-term equity anticipation securities). They are the same as short-term options except they offer opportunities over a longer period. LEAPS aren't available on every stock but are still readily available on the most widely held issues.

Exotic Options and Plain Vanilla Options

The initial call and puts options are sometimes called "plain vanilla." Don't be scared they are easy enough to follow.

A plain vanilla option is a standard option type. Having a simple expiration date and strike price, and that is it. With an exotic option, there may be other contingencies such as a knock-on options that become active when the stock hits a pre-determined price point. In other words...

Because of the versatility of options; there exist many types and variations. Non-standard options are called exotic options. These are either variation on the payoff profiles of the plain vanilla option or are wholly different products with "optionality" embedded in them.

Look this is a complex subject at times and it took me time to get to grips with the whole options trading ethos. All I can stress is until you are completely confident that you understand the intricacies of options trading, don't invest as you could lose a lot of money.

The following are ordinarily employed in the options trading process.

Strike Price

The strike price, also known as the exercise price, is the price at which an option holder - the buyer - may enter the underlying futures contract if they use the option. For call options, the strike price is the entry price at which one has the right to go long on the underlying commodity futures contract. For put options, this is the entry price at which one has the right to go short on the product.

Underlying Futures Contract

The fair futures contract that may be acquired or sold upon the exercise of the option. For example, an option on the December Silver futures contract is the right to buy or sell one December Silver futures contract.

Premium

The premium is a market-determined price (cost) of the option (which does not include commission and fees) that the buyer pays to purchase either a call option or a put option. It is a non-refundable cost that the option seller keeps, and is your maximum amount of risk in the market. Depending on your motive for purchasing the option, the premium represents either the cost of price protection (as a hedger) from adverse price movement, or the cost of opportunity (as a speculator) to profit potentially from a welcome price move with a pre-defined risk amount.

The option premium is quoted just like the price of the underlying futures contract; in cents, points, etc., but in some instances, the value of a "tick", or point, is different than the underlying futures contract.

Option premiums fluctuate daily due to market conditions. Just like with futures contracts, you profit if you first buy a call option at a particular premium (price), and then sell it back to the market at a higher price. If you monitor changes in an option's premium for at least two weeks, you may be able to buy your option at a reduced price.

Professional traders use various statistical analysis to compute what an option's premium should be. However, actual option premiums are determined through competitive bidding at the Exchange. Factors that determine the premium include:
* The current price of the underlying futures contract
* The volatility of the underlying futures contract
* The strike price concerning the current price of the underlying futures contract
* The amount of time remaining before the option expires
* Interest rates

For call options, the closer the strike price is to the underlying futures price, the more expensive the option is. For puts, the closer the strike price is to the futures price; the higher the option will be.

Options have two separate components that together define the option's premium. Exercising an option into the underlying futures contract will require you to post margin for the position, and you will also incur an additional cost from the commission to open the futures position.

Expiration Date

All options are assigned an expiration date after which they are no longer valid for trading purposes. This is the last day that the option may be exercised. Frequently, this date will be 2-4 weeks before the underlying futures contract's Last Trading Day (LTD), although some futures items synchronize the option expiration date with the futures contract LTD.

The farther out into the future an option's expiration date is, the more expensive the option will be (time = money). Any time before the option expiration date, an option purchaser can either exercise the option. (i.e., convert it to the underlying futures contract. this is at the strike price of the option being the entry point of the futures contract), liquidate the option (i.e., sell it back to the market), or let it expire worthless. You would only exercise an option if it were in-the-money (that is, the option is profitable). Option speculators rarely use their option. Instead, they will liquidate the option to either take profit when it has increased in value, or to prevent further time value loss (especially for expensive options).

If the option is either not exercised or liquidated by the option expiration date, and the option is not in-the-money, it will automatically expire worthless. If an option expires worthless, only the option seller benefits from the trade because they receive the full premium of the option when it was sold. The expired option also lets the option seller get out of their short option position without the need to initiate an offsetting transaction. In contrast, the seller of a futures contract can only get out of their position by offsetting it with another purchase or making delivery on the contract.

Automatic Exercise.
At the close of the option's expiration date, all in-the-money options are automatically exercised by BOT Clearinghouse. This means if the option you purchased is in-the-money when it expires, it will be converted to the underlying futures contract. If this does happen, make sure you establish a Stop-Loss Order with this futures position! However, it is best not to let this happen by liquidating the option a few weeks before the expiration date. So in summary, you buy either a call or put option to acquire it, and you liquidate your option to relinquish control of it.

Volatility
Volatility is a measure of how fast and how much the futures price changes and is expressed as a percentage - without regard to direction. It is considered the most important factors in selecting options for trading. Option prices become expensive when volatility is high (i.e., price movement is quick, and there are substantial changes in price magnitude). Conversely, option prices are less high when futures prices are quiet, and the market is not moving very much. The higher the volatility of a market, the more expensive an option will be.

An option with three months to expiration might command a higher premium in a volatile market than an option with six months to expiration in a stable market. Of the different ways to measure volatility, the two most important are implied volatility and statistical volatility.
* Implied volatility is used to determine the current market price of an option.
It uses the Black-Scholes formula to translate option premium into an accurate assessment of what traders "expect" the market to do. Also, it is a measure of trader sentiment. Option prices are affected most by changes in the underlying futures contract price, and second by changes in trader sentiment.
* Statistical volatility (also called historic volatility) is a descrip

tion of real price alters during a distinct time in the past.

Day Order

By default (and unless you stipulate otherwise), all orders you give to your broker are day orders. This means that if you place an order without any of the specifications described below, your order will apply for only that trading day. Each of the following orders may be submitted as a day order, or with other specified conditions. A common overriding condition available to traders is the good until canceled (also called 'GTC') order. When you specify GTC with your order, you are saying, "I want this order to continue from today onwards, until my order is either filled or I call my broker and cancel the order." Note: if you do GTC place orders, be certain you write it down, so you don't forget they exist. This will help you avoid unpleasant surprises when a forgotten order is filled - but the market's now going.

Stop Order

This is an order to buy at a price higher than the current market price, or to sell at a cost lower than the current market price. Stop orders may be used to buy into an up trending market or close your position in a down trending market. The stop order becomes a market order when the stop price is reached (touched). A stop order can be used as a risk management tool to protect open options. If price moves unfavorably (to the stop price), the stop order is executed, and the option position is liquidated, preventing any further loss of the option position.

Market-If-Touched Order

This order lets you buy at a price below the current market price or sell at a price higher than the current market price. When the specified price is "touched," in the opposite direction! This order becomes a market order. This order can only be placed on certain exchanges.

Market-On-Close Order

This order may only be executed in the closing price range at t he close of the trading day. This order is not available for all products.

Cancel/Replace Order
This order cancels out a previously entered order and replaces it with a new order.

Long Option
A long option is one that you buy. It can either be a long call or a long put. This is a limited risk option trade.

Short Option
A short option is one that you sell. It can either be a short call or a short put. This is an option trade with a risk that is not limited.

DAY 2 Types of Options

Index Options

Option trading is not restricted to individual stocks. The large commodity market is an option market that deals in all manners of commodities such as grain or cattle. There is also another type of investment known as index option trading.

An index is a listing of some different stocks that share something in common, and it represents the composite value of all of them. An example is the Dow Jones Industrial Average which represents the value of the 30 largest and most widely held industrial stocks on the New York Stock Exchange. The Pattern and Poor's 500 is a different index that represents 500 different stocks. These two well-known indices are frequently used to gauge the progress of the economy and the general health of the stock market. They are familiar to most people, even those with little or no interest in the market, as they are widely quoted on news broadcasts.

They represent just two of a large number. There are broad-based ones that reflect a wide range of widely different stocks, and there are ones that are very specific to a particular group. As the Dow Jones tracks industrial stocks, another index called The Morgan Stanley Biotech Index tracks 36 different stocks of companies engaged in biotech research. An index can list firms with similar goods, and even similar management styles. There are also a wide variety of foreign indices that reflect the composite value of foreign stocks.

An index may also be classified as to how it is weighted. Some regard every stock equally, and a price fluctuation in any stock in the index will have an impact on the index price no matter how large that individual stock's share of the index might be. Other indices "weight" the index based on the size of the company. In other words, small enterprises that experience even a large price change will not have as much impact on the index as a s light change in one of the most significant companies.

Index option trading is widespread in part because the risk is considered to be lower than with individual stock. This is partly because the index, representing a variety of stocks, is less likely to be subjected to the same adverse pressures that may cause an individual company to experience a very rapid decline in its value. The index is seen as much easier to subject to trend analysis, and this makes it an attractive part of most Mutual Fund portfolios.

There is another classification of indices that might be of interest to investors with certain social and environmental sensitivities. They are known as Ethical Indices as list stocks that satisfy certain criteria in their business operation. An example of one such index is the Wilderhill Clean Energy Index. Sadly, in the current market there is no direct connection between environmental sensitivity and profit, but with an Ethical Index, you can at least feel good about yourself while you make money, or even feel somewhat good if your investment turns out the opposite way.

Among the many investment opportunities that exist, option trading stands as both one of the most exciting and risky as well as one that offers some of the best chances for a substantial return. Learn all about options basics, stock and options trading, options strategies, and options pricing at http://www.option-trading-fortune.com

Commodity Options

Just like stock options, commodity option trading gives the investor the obligation to purchase or sell an underlying asset at a set value during a particular period. But in the case of commodity option trading, the underlying asset isn't stock, but a commodity.

A commodity is something more substantial than a stock; it is an actual product. Goods considered to be commodities are th ose that come up out of the earth and are in their raw, unprocessed form. Examples of products are things like wheat, oil, coffee and gold. All of these things have a value determined by the market, which is of coursed based on supply and demand. Most of us know that oil is a valuable commodity, and its value is likely to stay high unless we discover a new, cheaper source of energy to run our vehicles. Many commodities, however, can have much bigger fluctuations in price, which makes them an excellent investment opportunity.

Commodity option trading is a way for investors to be able to make a profit on the changeable value of products without massive investments or risk. An investor purchases the right to buy or sell the underlying commodity at the strike price within a given period. A profit can be made if the change in the value is enough to cover the premium paid for the option; if the change that is anticipated doesn't occur, the investor loses the premium.

Commodity option trading follows many of the same rules as stock options and has the same two basic types of transaction, the call, and the put. The call allows the holder of the option to buy the underlying asset at the strike price, while a put allows the option buyer to sell at the strike price.

Because the option is being purchased on goods that often don't exist yet - such as a harvest of wheat, it is often referred to as futures trading. Commodities can be very volatile - as can stocks, and it carries risks to the investor. Knowledge of the commodity market is vital to successful investing in this area.

Commodity option trading, like all the possibilities, is less risky than outright purchase of a product and requires a smaller investment. This makes it a great way for the average investor to get into the products market even if they don't have a lot of money with which to invest.

Forex Options

Option trading which is commonly associated with stock trading is popular in forex market too. There are two types of forex option trading. These are:

a) Call/ Put option, which operates just like the respective stock option.
B) SPOT or single payment option trading which offers greater flexibility to forex traders.

Call / Put or the traditional Options

In call / put forex option trading the buyer has a right to buy but not the obligation to purchase something from the option seller at a predetermined price and time. To quote an example, a trader might purchase an option to buy three lots of EUR/USD at 1.4000 in a month. This contract in forex terminology is known as an "EUR call/USD put." In case the price of EUR/USD falls to less than 1.4000, the option expires without the buyer NIL any amount. The buyer will only lose the premium amount. However, if EUR/USD increases to 1.5000, then the buyer can exercise his option and gain three lots of EUR/USD for only 1.4000. He can, in turn, sell these for a profit in the market.

FOREX options are traded over the counter. The traders can, therefore, pick the price and date on which the option is to be valid. There are two types of Call/put options American Style and European style.

Single Payment Options Trading (SPOT)

In SPOT forex option trading, the trader enters a scenario and lets it play out. To quote an example "EUR/USD will break 1.400 in 10 days will be input by the trader. He will obtain a premium quote also known as the option cost quote. If EUR/USD breaks 1.400, he will receive a payout.

Primarily in SPOT forex options, if the trader is right he accepts cash into his account. If not, he loses his premium. A distinct advantage of SPOT is that it allows a choice of scenarios. The actual decision is left to the trader depending upon his prediction of the market behavior.

In SPOT your option is automatically converted into cash when your option trade is thriving resulting receipt of a payout. One significant disadvantage of SPOT options is greater premiums compared to standard options.

Depending upon your unique needs you can choose the type of forex option trading you wish to engage in.

Forex market trading is no longer the domain of large institutions alone. Ordinary individuals like you and me can readily learn the basics of forex trading education and start trading profitably in the market.

Binary Options

Getting Started

Most trading platforms give two mild choices when it comes to binary trading: a put option and a call option. The put option is preferred if the trader considers that the price will decrease, while the call option is available for if they suppose that the price will rise. All traders need to decide their position based on any number of market factors, and numerous trading methods and algorithms can be used, which will be covered later.

Before choosing your position, you will be required to choose a trading platform through which you will be conducting all of your trades. Choosing the right broker to handle your finances is vital to the success of your trades, especially for beginning traders who need to make the most of all financial options. Not all brokers will be able to provide you with the same methods of trading, just like not all brokers will have the same limitations and returns available on their websites. For beginning traders, it is recommended not to worry about some of the more complicated binary trading methods. For now, choose a good brokerage that offers a high percentage of their returns, and see if there are any incentive programs offered that you can take advantage of.

Tips to Keep Remember

As with everything, there are various tips and tricks that beginning traders can keep in mind to increase their chances of profiting. Many of these tips are also designed to allow individuals to enjoy a much more comfortable trading experience, especially if they need a few rules of thumb to keep in mind as they trade. Eventually, as the trader becomes more and more experienced, they will be able to develop their trading methods and attitudes, designed specifically to complement their unique approach to trading. For now, however, just remembering a few of these simple tips can be enough to help most traders get a head start.

Leave Emotions Out of Your Trades

Perhaps the most important piece of advice to remember is never to rely on gut feelings or intuitive expectations. Trading binary options is not like gambling or any other mere money making process. While chance still plays a role in determining your profits, the vast majority of them will be determined by carefully analyzed indicators and effectively implemented strategies. Traders who rely on their instincts or any emotional connections with their finances will find that they will begin losing money in the long term, no matter what accidental profits they may secure at first.

Making emotionally driven trades is a vast mistake that, unfortunately, many entry level traders make. If your head is not clear and you are not thinking rationally, you will end up making trading mistakes. It is as simple as that. If you begin to feel frustrated or angry with your trades or become too excited after successful ones, it is important to take a step back, take a deep breath, and think about taking a break.

Think About Yourself as a Trader

The most prosperous traders are the individuals who know themselves and know what they want to get out of their trades. These are people who have looked into different types of options and have chosen to work with ones that match their personalities as traders. Most trades can be defined by the short, medium, and long term. Short term trades are identified by very quick transactions that take place in volatile environments, such as sixty-second and two-minute trades. Medium term trades refer to any transactions that can be made between five and fifteen minutes. Long term trades, as the name suggests, represent longer expiry periods, which can range anywhere from an hour to a day, depending on the broker.

As you can tell from the range, there is an approach to each typ e, one that helps define the trader. If you thrive in fast-paced situations and enjoy the risks that come with dealing with volatility, you will be better suited to work with short term trades. On the other hand, if you enjoy a lower degree of risk and plan on trading steadily for the long term, you may benefit from longer expiry options. Understanding your level of comfort and moving with it is crucial for all traders.

Start Slow

No matter how you plan on approaching the field, it is crucial for you to take your time and become familiar with your chosen strategy. Always start slow and become comfortable with your trading before you increase the size of your trades. Not only is this important in determining the success of your trades, but it can also help you make better decisions when it comes to different market situations. Whenever you have the chance, it is recommended for you to practice with some demo software to make sure that you know how to work with your strategy.

Analyze every trade you make and determine why they were successful or not. Just by reviewing your trades, you will be able to make much better decisions in the future. The more time that you are willing to spend analyzing your trades, the more successful you will be. The measure of a good trader is not in the sheer number of successful trades that they have made, but in their willingness to learn from their mistakes and continue improving.

Limit Your Losses Through Money Management Strategies

Everybody experiences a bad streak now and then, but not all traders know how to deal with it. They may end up making further poor decisions as a result, and, before they know it, they will end up losing a significant portion of their finances. Many people are familiar with the saying "Do not put all of your eggs in one basket." This saying applies to a variety of situations and is particularly important for traders to remember as well.

If you find that you are risking too much of your capital behind a single trade, take a step back and evaluate your finances. A good rule of thumb to remember is never to risk more than five percent of your current funds on any one trade. Many traders also strongly recommend taking a break for the day if you lose more than fifteen percent of your finances. No matter what, however, by keeping these money management strategies in mind, and adjusting them accordingly, you will still have a sizable portion of your capital available, even if things go wrong.

Diversify Your Strategies

In most other investment markets, traders will be strongly encouraged to diversify their investments. This is another good money management strategy, as it can allow them to spread their risk more evenly over a wider variety of commodities. It will ensure that they never lose too much of their investment, because where one product may fail, there will be others that are thriving. However, while this strategy may be useful with other types of trading, binary options can benefit from a different kind of diversification.

Binary options traders will be expected to be able to deal with a wide variety of diverse market situations, each of which can affect many commodities at varying times. It is for this reason that, instead of diversifying their assets, binary option traders are encouraged to expand their approaches and strategies. By understanding how different market climates can end up affecting their commodities, they will be able to act appropriately, without having to worry about taking breaks from their trades.

DAY 3 Trading Options

Placing the Order

How to Place An Order
Your broker will help you place your order. It's their job to help you - that's why you pay them a commission.

1. When you place an order, give your broker the following information:
* Your Account Number (if it's not your particular dealer)
* This is an Options order
* Whether you are buying a put option or a call option
* The number of options desired
* The Month and commodity
* The Strike Price
* The type of Order: Market, Limit, Stop, Day, Open, etc.
Unless you state otherwise, all orders given to your broker will be Day Orders and will expire at the completion of the trading day the order was given. No Open Orders are accepted on New York markets.

2. Listen to your broker when they verbally confirm your order. It is your responsibility to confirm that your broker has repeated your order correctly.

3. You must keep a written record of each order you give to your dealer. This will not only help you avoid "forgetting" about a trade, but it also gives you a way to monitor your trading results. A written record of all your trades also offers historic data about your trades which you can analyze for potential improvements you can make to your trading plan. Several forms are included with this trading course to help you track your option trades.

Market Order or Limit Order

Market Order
This order does not put any restriction on the price you are wil

ling to pay (if you are buying) or accept (if you are selling). It is used to get your order filled quickly. It is important to understand that the last option price quoted is only an indication of the prior market and is not necessarily the price you will receive when your market order is filled. The advantage using a market order is that when markets are trading, your order will be filled quickly. The disadvantage is that, in a highly volatile market, your order may be completed at a much higher or lower price than you anticipated.

Limit Order
This order lets you buy at a price lower than the current market price or to sell at a price higher than the current market price. This order is particularly useful if you are trying to stay within a certain price trading range. Limit orders are executed at the limit price, but if your order is filled, you are guaranteed that price or better. The disadvantage of the limit order is that your price may not be hit, and you may miss the market move. By default, the limit order is a day order (i.e., it only applies for that trading day) unless you specify other conditions (i.e., good until canceled, which means the order stands until it is either filled or canceled)

Time Restrictions

Time Restrictions refers to the amount of time remaining before the option expires. The likelihood of an option becoming profitable depends on the amount of time remaining until the option expires. The longer an option has until expiration, the more expensive it will be. This is because the underlying market has more time for the price to move, with a greater probability of moving substantially in one direction or another. Time value is a non-linear, decaying component of an option's value, so the loss of the option's time value will increasingly accelerate as time approaches the option's expiration date. This causes the value of the option to rapidly erode with the onset of the expiration date because the likelihood of a significant move occurring before expiration decreases. It's a good idea to liquidate expensive options three to four weeks before the option's expiration date to avoid the sharp time value loss.

DAY 4 Option Pricing

Pricing Basics

This chapter describes the technical aspects of option price behavior.

Greeks

The term Greeks is used to describe specific data values which are used by professional traders to analyze options. Top option traders know how changes in the Greeks will affect the profitability of their trades and adjust their trades accordingly. This information will help you define the risk of an option trade. The expected profit or loss of an option is based on changes in market price, time until expiration, as well as changes in implied option volatility.

Here is an example of why the Greeks are important. You purchase an over-priced call option. The futures market price rises steeply, but the value of your call option goes down. This is an example of the implied volatility being drained out of an option. In this case, the reduction in implied volatility (the adverse effect of Vega) was stronger than the price gain expected from market movement (the positive effect of the delta).

This can often happen after a major news event. After the news is out, the implied volatility of the option goes down because the "unknown" becomes" known". When this happens, speculating traders are no longer willing to pay a high premium for the option. Also, option sellers have less exposure to volatility risk, so their asking premium (selling price) also declines. This effect can be even more dramatic in thinly traded markets (i.e., markets with low volume) where few option sellers have greater control of the options market.

Option traders learn early in their career that a change in implied volatility can completely alter the option price. It is best to either buy low volatility, sell it when it's high, or use strategies t hat can neutralize the effects of this factor. When considering an option trade, you have to make assumptions about what you expect to happen to the Greeks as a trade commences.

Assuming that the implied option volatility or actual statistical volatility of the underlying futures price will stay unchanged is just as important as estimating that it will increase or decrease. Being wrong about this one factor can turn what you believe is a profitable trade into a losing trade. Some markets may exhibit a stable tenancy for implied volatility to increase with directional price moves. For example, implied volatility will increase in the S&P and stock indexes if the futures market price drops. Like-wise, volatility will increase in the grains or the softs if the futures price rallies.

There are several terms used to describe the relationship between the futures price and an option. These terms are referred to as the Greeks and are described below. Note: Except for Delta, the only way to get the Greeks for individual options or option spreads is to use an alternative software program such as OptionVue or from a broker who uses one. Manually calculating these values is too cumbersome.

Delta

Delta tells you how much of a change to expect - either an increase or decrease - in the option's premium when the underlying futures price moves. The projected price change in the option's premium is expressed as a percent of the variation in the price of a full futures contract.

Typically, option premiums do not modify cent-for-cent with shifts in the underlying futures price. This is because options that are in-the-money are more sensitive to changes in the underlying futures price than options that are either at-the-money or out-of-the-money. The price of a deep out-of-the-money option will move at a different magnitude than the price of an at-the-money option for the same price movement of the corresponding futures contract.

The delta value tells you how much the option price will change, percent-wise, when the futures price moves. At-the-money call options will have a delta of 0.50, meaning that you can expect the option to gain 50 percent of what the futures would gain on a price increase. A delta of 1.0 will cause a 1:1 movement between the futures price and the option premium.

However, the delta of an option is not fixed, but changes with variations in the futures price. As the futures price gets closer to the strike price, the value of delta increases. If the option goes in-the-money, the delta value will increase and vice versa. The further in-the-money that the option goes, the larger the delta value will be, causing the change in the option's premium to more closely mirror the change in the futures price.

Delta is continuously positive for calls and adverse for puts. Puts have a negative delta because puts increase in value when the futures price declines. If there is no change in implied volatility, you should expect a market decline to reduce the value of a long call option, just as would the passage of time. For combination positions involving multiple options, use the sum of all the deltas to get the combined delta for the entire position.

How To Calculate Delta
To calculate the delta of an option, you need the futures and option prices from two consecutive days. Calculate the change in the option price (premium) by subtracting yesterday's premium from today's premium. Do the same for the futures price, subtracting yesterday's close from today's close, to find the change in the futures price.

Gamma

The gamma tells you how much the option's delta will change when the underlying futures price changes. As the futures price moves, the delta changes, and gamma can tell you how much change to expect in the delta. If you start out with a delta of 0.50 in a call option, a rally in the underlying futures price will c ause delta to increase.

Gamma tells you how much you would expect Delta to change on a 100 point move in the futures. Just as we need to know how much we expect the price of an option to change according to its delta, we need to have an idea of how much the delta itself will change with market movement. Gamma will always be positive if you are a long premium in either calls or puts, and negative if short.

Theta
Theta
This value tells you how much the option's price will decline in one day if the future price does not move at all. It is a reflection of time value loss and is expressed as a dollar amount. Theta is a variable that can be affected either by changes in the futures price, time left until expiration and changes in implied volatility.

All other things being equal, long options decline in value as time passes, and this effect accelerates as time gets closer to the option expiration date. Since any option that is in-the-money has intrinsic value that is equal to its position beyond its strike price, any premium value beyond that is the time premium. Because all time premium will be gone at option expiration, theta tells you how much of that premium you expect to lose on a long option (or gain on a short option) on a daily basis. Options or combination positions which have several months of time value remaining until expiration will have a little premium loss from time decay. The theta value will be positive for short option positions and negative for long positions.

Vega
This value tells you how much the option price will change if implied volatility changes. It is the "sensitivity" of the option's price to volatility. Vega is expressed as a dollar amount. A positive Vega indicates that a rise in implied volatility will benefit y

our position. Vega tells you how much you can expect the theoretical value of an option to change based on a 1 percent change in implied volatility. For example, if the implied volatility of an option rises from 20 % to 30 %, it has risen 10 percent, regarding calculating the Vega. However, when comparing the implied volatility of an option that is at 30 percent to one that is trading at 20 percent, the first one has a 50 percent higher implied volatility.

Some facts about the Greeks
All of the Greeks are values which reflect a point in time. Because they are dynamic, they will change with the passage of time, if implied volatility changes. Because the Greeks are "related", if the Delta changes, the Gamma, Theta, and Vega will change too. This trading knowledge and experience can be very helpful in making some important assumptions about how a trade will respond in the future.

Day 5 Buying Selling, Exercising Options

When using options in the stock market, the underlying asset is 100 shares of a specific stock or exchange-traded fund (ETF). Options are also available on some broad-based indexes. When entering an order to buy or sell options, your broker electronically sends the order to one of the option exchanges where the order is executed. This is essentially the same method used to buy or sell stock.

If you ever elect to exercise an option, notify your broker, who takes care of the rest of the process. There is nothing else for the option owner to do – it is an automatic process once you exercise the option. If you trade an option and later are allowed an exercise notice, you are notified about this transaction (it is an operation because when assigned, you either buy or sell stock at the strike price) by your broker.

The notification arrives before the market opens the next trading day. The assignment occurs overnight. If you are designated an exercise notice on a call option, 100 shares will have been removed from your account and replaced with cash (100 * strike price; less commissions) by the time you see your account information on the following business day. It is the same as if you sold 100 shares overnight.

If assigned to a put option, 100 shares appear in your account, and the cash to pay for those shares (plus commissions) has been removed. Again, you bought 100 shares while the markets profit. In other words, there is no notice of a pending assignment. Once you are notified, the assignment is permanent (it cannot be reversed without making a new stock trade to offset the assignment). Most exercises and assignments occur at expiration, but it is possible for an option owner to exercise an option before expiration. It does not happen very often, but there is one exception when a call option is deep in the money.

Sometimes an option is exercised one day before the stock goe s ex-dividend. That happens because option owners do not collect dividends. Only stockholders do. Thus, the call owner who wants the dividend must exercise the option and convert it to stock.

DAY 6 Option Strategies

Options are versatile investment tools, and there are many ways to use them. Some methods are highly speculative. Some are conservative. I recommended learning conservative strategies, particularly in the beginning of your option trading career.

Later, if you must, you can attempt more aggressive methods.
I believe that traditional strategies are beneficial in helping the average individual investor earn additional profits from an investment portfolio. Thus, I limit the lessons that I teach to strategies that come with limited risk.

The strategies used most often during my trading career include (additional details below):
-- Writing covered calls
-- Selling naked puts
-- Credit and debit spreads (Vertical spreads)
-- Calendar Spreads
-- Iron Condors

This listing is not exhaustive since there are many more strategies that traders use. This list is suitable for the newer trader. Just know that because of their versatility, options can be combined into very complex strategies used only by professional traders.

Once you understand how a few strategies work, you will have an excellent idea as to the type of policy that best suits your investing objectives, your tolerance for risk, and most importantly, your character traits (i.e., lack of greed and good discipline).
However, any lengthy discussion of these strategies is beyond the scope of this book. The short descriptions below are designed to give readers an idea of what can be done with options.

Writing Covered Calls

This involves buying 100 shares of stock and selling one call op tion. The word 'covered' refers to the fact that when selling any option, there is always the possibility that you will be assigned an exercise notice. As mentioned earlier, when you are assigned an exercise notice on a call option, you are required to deliver (i.e., sell) 100 shares to the person who used.

When you already own the shares, then the call option is 'covered' – meaning that you own the shares, and they can be delivered. When you do not own the shares, then the option is considered to be 'uncovered' or 'naked.' When that happens, you still must deliver the shares. If your account is allowed to sell stock short, then your position will change from being short call options to being short 100 shares of the underlying stock for each call option that was exercised. Most brokers do not allow novice option traders to write (sell) open calls, so you are not expected to run into this problem.

When adopting this strategy, the trader owns a slightly bullish position. The primary risk is that the stock price will decline sharply. No matter what else happens, you, the covered call writer, gets to keep the premium collected from selling the call option (minus your broker's commission). The best possible result is achieved when the stock price increases – giving the trader a capital gain. There is a maximum possible profit, and that occurs when the stock price is higher than the strike price ($85 in this example) when expiration arrives.

When the stock is less than the strike price (and most of the time when it equals the strike price) at expiration, it expires and becomes worthless. You keep your stock and may write another call option with a later expiration date. When the stock is above the strike price at expiration, then the option owner exercises and pays $85 per share. Thus, your profits are capped, or limited. You cannot sell your shares at any price above $85.

Selling Naked Puts

This is about as simple as a strategy can be. However, you mus t be aware that large losses are possible. Translation: If you would consider buying 200 shares of stock, then it is appropriate to sell two puts because if you are assigned an exercise notice, you would own 200 shares. If you stray from this rule, there will remain the possibility of hurting your trading account. There are two primary plans when selling naked put options:

- The investor is willing to buy a stock at the strike price. Note: The final cost of buying the shares equals the strike price, minus the premium collected from the put sale.

- The trader has no interest in buying stock. He/she is looking to earn a profit from the trade. That is accomplished by closing the position when satisfied with the profit. Sometimes you may seek the maximum possible profit and allow the puts to expire worthless. At other times, the stock price may decline, and you may fear to lose too much money. You solve that dilemma. The best choice is to cover the position and accept a loss (before it becomes a large loss).

Vertical Spreads

This represents an inventive method for selling options – but with reduced risk and reduced profit potential. Why would anyone be willing to make a trade with a smaller maximum benefit? Because the sum that can be lost when an unforeseen event occurs is so significant that it becomes worthwhile to eliminate that possibility in return for accepting less potential gain.

If you accept this idea, then you are already on your way to understanding how to manage risk when trading. It is my hope that the most crucial factor that determines any trader's future success or failure is the trader's ability to manage risk. In that spirit, I recommend adopting strategies with limit risk Calendar Spreads (also known as Time Spreads) The calendar is composed of two options – one bought and the other sold.

Calendar Spreads

The calendar is composed of two options – one bought and the other sold. The underlying asset and the strike price are identical, but the expiration dates are different. The theory is that when the shorter-term option is covered (either by expiring worthless or being purchased in a closing transaction), the trader can sell the longer-term option at a premium that is higher than the original debit paid for the spread. The difference between the purchase and sale price (as with all trades) represents a profit or loss.

How the calendar spread earns a profit:

1. Time decay.

- Options are a wasting asset and when all else remains unchanged, lose value every day.
- Shorter-term options decay more rapidly than longer-term options.
- An option whose strike price is very near that of the underlying stock has more time premium than other options. Translation: When the stock is near the strike price of the calendar spread, the position earns the highest profit.

Iron Condor

This is a fancy name for a simple idea:
- A position consisting of two vertical spreads
- Both spreads use the same underlying asset
- Both spreads expire at the same time (Dec 19, 2014)
- One spread consists of calls (strikes 1250 and 1260)
- One spread consists of puts Strikes 1140 and 1150)
- Both spreads are credit spreads
- Position Objective

Earn money from the passage of time When the iron condor works: As time passes, and INDX remains far away from 1150 and 1250, all options lose value due to time decay. In fact, when enough time passes (expiration arrives) and the options remain out of the money (that means INDX is above 1150 and below 1250) then all four options become worthless. Remember that you sell two vertical spreads when constructing an iron condor, and the cash collected from that sale represents the maximum profit that can be achieved.

Iron Condor Risk: When INDX does not remain comfortable between the strike prices of the options sold (1150 and 1250), then one portion of the iron condor position results in a monetary loss. This is clearly seen in the risk graph. When INDX moves through 1150 on a market decline, or through 1250 on a rally, the value of the options that were sold increases so much – that the trader loses money. [Yes, the put spread becomes almost worthless when INDX moves above 1250, but the loss on the call spread is far greater than the gain on the put spread.] The good news is that risk is limited.

As you will understand when trading options it is important to trade with limited risk and I encourage you to avoid all option positions that come with unlimited risk (selling naked calls, for example). One further point on risk: Having "limited risk" is not enough. You will want to learn all about managing risk so that all positions have an acceptable (to you and your comfort zone) amount of risk and an acceptable potential reward (profit). It takes a bit of experience to get a good feel for how to accomplish that, but please keep in mind that it is easy to make money with options. The problem is that it is also easy to lose money with options and all traders have to avoid losing too much money on any given trade. That is the only way to be assured that losses do not overwhelm profits.

Conclusion

In summary thousands of small retail traders are making a living, and some a fortune, from trading options and you are eager to take a shot at it too, aren't you? So, what are some of the things you must know to master options trading?

What are stocks and shares and how they work?

Stock options are derivatives of shares. This means that you need to know what shares are in the first place to understand the role of options and how options work. In fact, you will need to be a master of stock and shares behavior before you could be a master of options trading because options are merely tools that help you exploit these stock and shares behavior profitably.

What options are

It sounds like common sense but most options traders start out thinking options are just "another stock" which you simply buy low and sell high. Those who jump into their first options trade like this usually get a shock of their lives when they either realize that options don't quite move the way they expect them to move and don't quite behave the way they expect them to behave. Knowing how options work and what their underlying mechanisms are, the logic behind call and put options are the basic knowledge all master options traders need.

Options strategies

The real magic of options trading lies not in simply buying call options for stocks expected to go up or buying put options for stocks expected to go down. The actual magic of options trading lies in the universe of options strategies which allows you to profit not only from an upwards or downwards market but even in a neutral or volatile one. You probably won't be able to learn, practice and master each and every of the hundreds of options strategies but you should have at least one or two options strat egies for each class that you are entirely familiar with and have paper traded so that you have a weapon for each market condition.

Technical Analysis

Technical analysis is particularly important for options trading as it is through technical analysis that you can make trend analysis to know what class of options strategy to apply in the first place. Technical analysis is paramount in options trading also due to entry and exit timing which is vital in options trading where there is a fixed expiration. Technical analysis has been used over the decades as a tool for precision entry and exit and is now an important tool in options trading.

Options Greeks

Options Greeks are the mathematical components that define how a particular option would behave in response to factors such as changes in the price of the underlying stock, changes in volatility, changes in interest rate and time decay. An intimate understanding of all the options Greeks allows you to understand better and predict the behavior of an options position. It also allows you to make difficult adjustments to your options position to create a payoff profile that conforms to the exactly predicted behavior of the price of the underlying asset.

Delta Neutral Trading

Delta neutral trading is the ability to tweak a position's delta status to a level that is zero or almost zero such that small volatilities in the price of the underlying asset do not affect the value of the overall position. When delta neutral trading is performed correctly, it could even be used as a hedge which profits no matter which direction the price of the underlying asset breaks out into next. This can only be accomplished by a blend of call options, put options, the underlying asset and even futures. Different situations require a different approach to delta neutral hedging, and that is why it takes a strong knowledge in all of th ese instruments to do delta neutral trading well.

Mastering all of the above will allow you to realize your dream as a master options trader and be able to make a living from trading options. Are you able to master all of the above?

www.ingramcontent.com/pod-product-compliance
Lightning Source LLC
Chambersburg PA
CBHW070105210526
45170CB00013B/752